del
75º

RALPH EARL, RECORDER FOR AN ERA

It is the treating of the commonplace
with the feeling of the sublime that
gives art its true power.

—JEAN FRANÇOIS MILLET[1]

Ralph Earl

RECORDER FOR AN ERA

by
LAURENCE B. GOODRICH

THE STATE UNIVERSITY OF NEW YORK

PICTURE CREDITS

Pictures in this book appear by permission from their owners, who provided the photographs reproduced, with the following exceptions:

Frick Art Reference Library, New York—Drawing, page xi, and Figures 3, 25, 38.

National Portrait Gallery, London—Figures 12 and 20.

The Metropolitan Museum of Art, New York—Figure 29.

*To
Lois*

FOREWORD

Pursuit of a painter—an adventure in itself—can be attended by noteworthy events and the formation of valued acquaintanceships unlikely to be brought about in any other way. The search becomes additionally engaging with an artist like Earl, who operated on both sides of the Atlantic during an exceptionally colorful period of history.

It is with both pleasure and a sense of indebtedness to many persons who manifested interest in this project and generously assisted therewith, that the writer of these pages recalls happy experiences that marked the course of his research. The list of all who contributed would require considerable space. However, certain isolated incidents deserve mention. These include an inspection of the Earl and Trumbull paintings in Yale University's rich art collection under the gracious guidance of Josephine Setze; the hospitality of Sir Gyles Isham, Bart., who welcomed the author and his wife to stately Lamport Hall, Northampton, to view a family portrait there; a similar visit with Mrs. Clevland Onslow in Ripley, Surrey, where a hitherto unknown Earl was identified.

The ready cooperation of two other persons resulted in the locating of a pair of Earls in Switzerland. When A. H. Scott-Eliot, Keeper of Prints and Drawings in the Royal Library at Windsor Castle, was asked if she had knowledge of any paintings by Earl, she recalled having seen works bearing his signature some twenty-five years before when she went with friends through Plazzo de Salis at Bondo, Switzerland. Count Charles de Salis, in answer to a letter of inquiry, wrote that, though he was unaware of Earls in his collection, the author might explore the plazzo, should his travels take him to Switzerland. Thus one person's remarkable memory and another's willingness to open his house to a stranger combined to bring to light the charming portraits of the Drake sisters. At a later meeting with the Count in London, the provenance of these works was discussed.

This study has entailed voluminous correspondence with libraries, historical societies, museums, art historians, and other institutions and individuals. Perhaps most frequent demands were made of Kingsley Adams, Director, National Portrait Gallery, London; C. Andrew Humeston, Secretary, New Milford (Connecticut) Historical Society; and William L. Warren, Director, The Stowe-Day Foundation, Hartford, Connecticut—all of whom responded generously. For reading the manuscript and offering suggestions thereon, grateful acknowledgment is made to Catherine Fennelly, Director of Research and Publications, Old Sturbridge Village, Massachusetts, and Louis Jones, Director, New York State Historical Association. The friendly encouragement of James A. Frost and of Chandler McC. Brooks, both of State University of New York, has been warmly appreciated.

Thanks are extended to museums and individual owners for permissions granted to reproduce their Earl paintings.

To his wife, Lois S. Goodrich, whose interest lent zest to this undertaking and whose companionship increased immeasurably the pleasure derived from the travel involved, the author dedicates this slim volume.

Ralph Earl.

RALPH EARL, RECORDER FOR AN ERA

On a wind-swept hilltop in the old cemetery at Bolton, Connecticut, surrounded by weathered gravestones dating back to the early 1700's, a red sandstone monument was erected in 1935, Connecticut's tercentenary year. The inscription reads:

> IN MEMORY OF RALPH EARL
> One of the foremost portrait painters in
> America of his time. Born at Shrewsbury,
> Massachusetts, May 11th, 1751, he studied in
> London under his countryman Benjamin
> West; was an exhibitor in the Royal Academy;
> and, upon returning to his native country
> in 1786, painted chiefly in Connecticut.
> His portraits of American patriots include
> three signers of the Declaration of Indepen-
> dence—Roger Sherman, Governor Oliver
> Wolcott, Sr., and William Floyd—and those
> of Chief Justice Oliver Ellsworth, General
> Baron von Steuben, Colonel Samuel Talcott,
> Colonel Benjamin Tallmadge, Major Moses
> Seymour, and the Honorable George Wyllys.
> His death here in Bolton, August 16th, 1801,
> was recorded by the Rev. George Colton
> (1736-1812), and he was presumably
> buried here in an unmarked grave.[2]

One detail of this statement is now known to be inaccurate: later findings have established that Earl returned to America in May, 1785. Nevertheless, behind the brief words lies a story of one of the most gifted, perhaps the most misunderstood, and for long the most neglected of American artists. His career is unique and paradoxical. Considered the earliest of American painters of historical scenes and a pioneer landscapist, he lived in a day when only portraiture was in vogue. A Tory, he fled to England in the first years of the Revolution, only to return after the war to become Connecticut's outstanding painter of Revolutionists. Promptly relegated to oblivion after his death, he was rediscovered early in the present century and today is ranked among the most brilliant and historically important artists of the land.

For the works of Earl—more intimately than those of any other painter—bring us today a realistic view of post-Revolutionary America. He did more than portray handsome contemporaries with exceptional insight into character. He did more than depict their eighteenth-century dress with remarkable skill, his deft brushwork conveying the luster of a silk gown, the crispness of a starched ruffle, the transparency of a sheer muslin fichu, the richness of a brocaded vest. His pictures show people in their own houses, surrounded by their furniture, caressing their pets, pursuing their customary occupations. Behind them appear enchanting glimpses of identifiable scenes—countryside, seashore, tree-shaded river, village with church spire, harbor with shipping. For during the closing 1700's—spent largely in the towns and country houses of New York, Connecticut, Massachusetts, and Vermont—the itinerant Earl produced a glowing pictorial record of an era. Small wonder that great interest attaches to the tantalizing fragments of information about his career that have so far come to light.

Of the boyhood of Earl, we know little. Son of Ralph and Phebe (Whittemore) Earle, his birth on May 11, 1751, is recorded in both Leicester and Shrewsbury, Massachusetts. The latter being his parents' residence at the time, Shrewsbury is considered the more likely birthplace. The family, farmers and craftsmen, had prospered in Worcester County since the great-grandfather, Ralf Earle, came there from Rhode Island in 1717. Although the usual spelling of the family name seems for generations to have been *Earle, Earll* appears in the birth record of Ralph in Shrewsbury. For reasons best known to themselves, Ralph and his artist brother James signed themselves *Earl.*

The painter's father moved early to Leicester. Here young Ralph must have attended the school erected on the common in 1736, a structure which Emory Washburn describes with feeling as "the perfection of discomfort and ill-adaptation to its purpose." "The house," he writes in *Historical Sketches of the Town of Leicester,* "was warmed —so far as such a thing was possible—by a huge wood-fire built in an immense fireplace; around which some of the scholars were always gathered to warm their feet, which grew cold again the moment they had taken their seats. . . . These seats, benches, were narrow and intolerably hard. . . . The pupil wrote, ciphered, and studied without ever associating anything but aching limbs and stiffened joints with the acquisition of a schoolboy's knowledge."[3]

A number of guesses have been ventured as to where Ralph and his brother James, who himself became a portraitist of lesser merit, may have secured early instruction in painting. Alan Burroughs[4] suggests Samuel King of Newport, teacher of Gilbert Stuart and

Washington Allston. There are points of similarity between some of King's works and some of Earl's. William Johnston is mentioned as a possibility by Samuel W. Green.[5] All of which is sheer conjecture. Earl may at first have been wholly self-taught. The primitive character of the works of his first American period, though charming, betrays little technical finesse. Nevertheless, by 1774, he had established his own studio in New Haven.

Here his friend, the young engraver Amos Doolittle, kept a shop on the present site of one of Yale's buildings on the green.[6] His portrait (Figure 15) is among Earl's earlier works. Compared with later paintings, it seems heavy and rather crude. Yet the purposeful face is interesting in a dark, forbidding way.

Hearing of the armed clashes that opened the Revolution early in 1775, the two young men betook themselves the following summer to Lexington and Concord. According to Doolittle's account,[7] Earl sketched the scenes of recent action, calling upon his friend to pose for various persons appearing therein. ". . . When he [Earl] wished to represent one of the Provincials as loading a gun, crouching behind a stone wall when firing on the enemy, he would require Mr. D. to put himself in such a position," records Barber. Having made a series of drawings, the pair returned to New Haven, where Earl completed in his studio the four historical paintings from which Doolittle made his popular set of engravings. Thanks to the keen eye and superior sleuthing of William Sawitsky,[8] one of these pictures, *A View of the Town of Concord* (Figure 3), was located some years ago. It is obviously too unwieldy to have been produced "on the spot" as claimed. Though a youthful work and not without faults, it is superior to Doolittle's crude engravings, which distort men, reverse the perspective of buildings, and make walls look paper-thin. These plates were Doolittle's "first attempt at art"—and look it.

Evidently some months were required to bring this project to completion, for it was not until December 13, 1775, that an advertisement appeared in the *New Haven Journal* asserting that "Four different Views of the Battles of Lexington and Concord, &c., on the 19th April, 1775," were "this Day Published and to be sold at the store of *Mr. James Lockwood*, near the College, in New Haven."[9] After listing the views, the statement concludes thus: "The above four Plates are neatly engraven on Copper, from original paintings taken on the spot. Price, six shillings per set for the plain ones, or eight shillings, colored." Today, this series is virtually priceless. Except for Paul Revere's prints of the Boston Massacre in 1770 and of the British in Boston in 1774, the Earl-Doolittle prints may be considered the first series of historical

FIGURE 1

A VIEW OF THE TOWN OF CONCORD

This is Plate II from the series of four engravings on copper based on Earl's historical paintings of the battles of Lexington and Concord. Issued December 13, 1775, they have the distinction of being the first prints published in Connecticut.

The impressions were available both untinted and colored. One of the latter was used for the accompanying reproduction, a fact that accounts for the over-all grayness of tone. The original is brilliantly colored by hand. On the margin above the picture appear the number and title of the plate. Beneath it are notes identifying the two officers as Major Pitcairn and Colonel Smith "viewing the Provincials" who were mustering on an east hill. "Companies of Regulars marching into Concord" are seen beyond the cemetery wall. On the far side of the pond is a "Detachment destroying the Provincial Stores." At the extreme left is the "Meetinghouse" and at the extreme right the "Townhouse." The building facing the cemetery entrance later became Wright Tavern.

While one cannot much admire Doolittle's amateurish handling of perspective and human proportions, this engraving, with the others that constitute the series, is an item of prime interest and historical importance.

Inscribed: A. Doolittle, Sculpt.
18 x 13 inches
The New York Public Library
The I. N. Phelps Stokes Collection

4

engravings ever published in America. As such, they have been pronounced "possibly the choicest of all American historical items."[10]

The often-expressed notion that Earl marched with Colonel Benedict Arnold's recruits and participated in the battles of Lexington and Concord is not only without supporting evidence but also incompatible with known facts. Young Earl was evidently an unwavering Tory, although his father was a captain in the Rebel army, his brother Clark served as a Minute Man, and several cousins fought and died for American independence. The high material cost Ralph paid for his loyalty to George III is a matter of record; the tragic spiritual cost cannot be doubted.

In Leicester in 1774, Earl had married his cousin, Sarah Gates of Worcester. A daughter, Phebe, was born to them on January 25 of the next year. But the marriage was a failure. In conflicting testimony given forty years later, the former Mrs. Earl—by then Mrs. Oliver Pierce—first asserted that she resided with Ralph "as his wife whilst he lived in this country." In the same deposition, she said, "We began to keep house in November 1776 in Newhaven [sic] about two years after we were married, and continued until the May following, which is all the time we kept house together."[11] While is seems impossible to reconcile these statements with each other, they indicate a sufficiently unsatisfactory domestic situation. A second child, John, was born in Worcester, May 13, 1777, the same month the parents broke up housekeeping, according to the mother. Presumably Sarah returned to her father's house. The contemptuous attitude of her kin is revealed by the assertion that Earl "was a Tory and skedaddled, leaving her behind," a statement made in the genealogy of the Gates family (1898). That the skedaddling was not by his own choice will be seen presently. One feels sure that the Earles were as critical as the Gateses. The effect on the marriage of this climate of disapproval can be imagined. Whatever Sarah's views at the time, the fact that she married again indicates that she divorced her Loyalist husband. All efforts to find records of the dates of her divorce and remarriage have so far been fruitless.

Though without date and signature, Earl's arresting portrait of Roger Sherman (Figure 2) is assumed to have been painted about this time (c. 1775). Primitive in style and far from flawless in draftsmanship, it is nevertheless a powerful study of this granite shoemaker-statesman, whose signature already appeared on the Declaration of Independence and would soon be appended to both the Articles of Confederation and the Federal Constitution. Though Earl later produced portraits more gracious and decorative, his startling grasp of character was never to be more surely asserted than in this great likeness of Connecticut's eminent citizen.

But clouds of the Revolution were fast gathering about young Earl. Refusing to accept a commission in his father's regiment, he was disinherited. Later, when he was summoned before a Committee of Safety in New Haven and again declined to cooperate with the Rebels, he was given the choice of quitting Connecticut or going to prison. He pretended to leave the colony, but actually sought refuge with Tory friends in "a remote part of the Province." In March, 1776, hearing of Rebel plans to cut off a party of the King's troops from the east end of Long Island, he and confederates dispatched a messenger some thirty miles by boat to apprise the British of the plot. The warning enabled the Redcoats to repulse the attack.

The following April, Earl was again haled before the Committee of Safety under suspicion of corresponding with the enemy. The artist states that but for "the respect which they paid his Father as an Officer of High Rank in their Army," he would certainly have been executed. Instead, he was again allowed the alternative of prison or banishment. Realizing his extreme danger, Earl resolved to embark for England at the earliest opportunity. That opportunity presented itself when he fell in with one Captain I. Money, Quartermaster General to Burgoyne's army. With his help, Earl secured safe passage from Providence to Newport disguised as the Captain's servant. Thence they sailed for England, which they reached in April, 1778.

This dramatic series of events is detailed in a petition found in 1949 by John Marshall Phillips[12] among manuscripts in the Public Record Office, London. It was addressed on January 28, 1779, to "the right Honble The Lords Commissioners of the Treasury." After representing how seriously his loyalty to the Crown had damaged the petitioner's prospects and urging the "utmost Distress" of his present circumstances, the document closes with these words:

> Therefore Your Petitioner humbly requests that Your Lordships will consider the Hardships under which Your Petitioner now Labors and grant unto him such Relief and Support as the present Necessity of his Case requires and as to Your Lordships shall seem meet.

If this petition brought results, they are not on record.

However mistaken Earl may have been in his attitude toward American independence, one cannot but respect the steadfastness with which he maintained his views despite persuasion, danger, and personal loss.

Upon his arrival in England, it is likely that Earl made immediate contact with his fellow countryman Benjamin West, whose establishment in London had already proved a hospitable haven for more than one aspiring American artist. His initial sojourn in the capital was but brief, however. Before the close of 1779, he was painting his delightful portraits of the Carpenter children at Aldeby in Norfolk (Figure 4). Though more colorful than *Roger Sherman*, they show little relaxation of the ingenuous angularity seen in all the artist's earlier efforts. This attractive characteristic was soon to be modified. Direct contact with the works of Gainsborough, Reynolds, West, Romney, and other exemplars of the English grand manner could not fail to make Earl a more knowing technician. His pictures took on a more painterly grace, but retained his distinctive honesty, directness, and vitality.

Four years after the Carpenter portraits, he was entering his bluff *Colonel George Onslow, M.P.* (Figure 5) in the Royal Academy exhibition of 1783. It is probable that this work, only recently identified,[13] was done in 1782. It hung for generations in Desborough House, Onslow's stately country manor at Ripley in Surrey.

Although the year 1783 may not have been an exceptionally active one for Earl, we have more data concerning it than any other during his English period. He had evidently returned to London and probably to West. Catalogue notes[11] on his two entries in the Royal Academy exhibit opening in May, show him lodging in Hatton Garden and Leicester Fields. At these addresses or at 12 Bowling Street, he must have painted *Rear Admiral Richard Kempenfelt* (Figure 7),[15] *Lady Williams and Child*, and *A Master in Chancery Entering the House of Lords* (Figure 8)—all of which are dated 1783. Toward the end of the year, we find him at the Misses Dutton's school at Windsor, Berkshire, painting *Sophia Isham* (Figure 6). The date also appears on the luminous *Marianne Drake* (Figure 9), his likeness of the elder daughter of Sir Francis William Drake of Hillingdon Place, Middlesex.[16]

From details contained in a short letter written by Earl from Windsor on September 23, 1784, to Dr. Joseph Trumbull, a young American apothecary visiting in London, one can draw certain conclusions concerning the artist's activities and connections both before and after this date.[17] Therein he twice alludes to Benjamin West in a manner at once casual and intimate. The Sawitskys point out that during the late 1770's and early 1780's, West, as favorite painter to George III, regularly accompanied the royal family to Windsor, the king's preferred place of residence. From London, there went with West members of his family and some of his pupils. Completing the circle were certain practising painters who, while not formally studying with West, enjoyed his friendship, were influenced by his example, and benefited from his contacts with the aristocratic and the well-to-do. Among these followers was Earl. Although his name is not to be found on the roster of pupils at West's academy, it is reasonable to assume that Earl depended on the great man's help for a considerable length of time. The *Sophia Isham* and the Trumbull letter prove Earl's presence in Windsor two years in succession. It seems clear that a number of his best English portraits were produced there.

Earl's marriage to Ann Whiteside (Figure 13) of Norwich, England, is assumed to have occurred about 1784, a union declared bigamous by scandalized reporters ever since. The artist may well have been blameless, however. A tradition among descendants of both Sarah Gates Earl and Ann Whiteside Earl lends support to the conjecture that he believed his first wife dead. On the other hand, she may already have divorced him. As to the second wife, a persistent but totally false story maintains that she was deserted by a faithless husband, who absconded to America, leaving her with their two children: Mary Ann Earl and Ralph Eleazer Whiteside Earl. The absurdity of this gossip was established recently by the discovery in Massachusetts papers [18] for May, 1785, of news items listing "Mr. Earl and lady" among passengers just arriving at Boston "in 30 days from England" on the ship *Neptune*. Added evidence of the year of crossing is the portrait of Captain Silas Talbot, completed in Providence, Rhode Island, about October, 1785.[19] Since Mary Ann was born in 1787 and Ralph E. W. in 1788, it would be patently impossible for a father, no matter how irresponsible, to abandon them in 1785. Although Earl was unquestionably much on the move and quite possibly saw his family but seldom, there is no evidence of desertion. Is this misrepresentation another example, one wonders, of the kind of detraction suffered after the Revolution by those who chose to support the losing side?

At an undetermined date, Mrs. Earl settled in Troy, New York, recognizing, perhaps, the futility of trying to stay with her husband on his roving pursuit of patrons. Here, she was identified with the Episcopal church. D.A.R. lineage records show that Mary Ann grew up to marry Colonel Benjamin Higbee of Troy; while Ralph E. W. married the niece of Mrs. Andrew Jackson, lived at the White House and the Hermitage, and painted successive likenesses of Old Hickory.

With an exuberance typical of most press notices relating to Earl, the New York *Independent Journal: or General Advertiser* for November 25, 1785, announced, "Last Sunday arrived in town from England, by way of Boston, Mr. Ralph Earl, a native of Massachusetts; he has passed a number of years in London under those distinguished and most celebrated Masters in Painting, Sir Joshua Reynolds, Mr. West, and Mr. Copley. The gentleman now proposes to enter upon his profession in this city, where a specimen of his abilities may be seen on calling at Mr. Rivington's No. 1 Queen Street."[20] Self-promotion through the press being common practice in his day, Earl is assumed to have composed this item.

Earl seems never to have lacked for sitters. It was at this time that he painted the striking likeness of Major General Frederick William Augustus, Baron von Steuben (Figure 18), the former aide-de-camp to Frederick the Great who volunteered his services without compensation to the American Revolutionary cause and rendered unique assistance thereto.

However, the artist had apparently already developed spendthrift ways and a taste for drink. In consequence, we presently find him confined for debt within the gray stone walls of New York's city prison. Hearing of his plight, the ever out-going Alexander Hamilton, then a successful New York lawyer but soon to be Washington's Secretary of the Treasury, proposed a plan to relieve the impecunious painter. At her husband's suggestion, Mrs. Hamilton (Figure 19) posed for her portrait in the jail.[21] Some of the Hamiltons' friends did likewise. Among these was probably handsome Matthew Clarkson (Figure 20), the young New Yorker whose military gallantry and high social position had made him a leader in state and city politics. His superb likeness, signed and dated 1787, manifests exceptional mastery of technique and penetrating understanding of character.

Earl remained in prison until some time in 1788. On January 21 and again on January 28 of that year, the New York *Morning Post and Daily Advertiser* carried a petition addressed to the "creditors of Ralph Earl, an insolvent debtor," requesting that they show cause why his estate should not be attached to satisfy his debts. Whatever the settlement, the artist was in Greenfield, Connecticut, later the same year, producing the first of his series of paintings of the Bradley family.

Earl's artistic reputation stands securely on the distinguished array of Connecticut portraits he did during his second American period. At quiet, elm-shaded New Milford in 1789, he painted the handsome Boardman brothers—Daniel and Elijah—elegant young Federalists, prosperous in business and prominent in politics of the new-born republic. The portrait of Daniel (Figure 24) is noteworthy for the exquisite background view of the town and the valley of the Housatonic. Elijah (Figure 25) is represented in his dry goods store. Clearly Earl had evolved from his mixed American and English labors the frank and realistic style that gives his canvases such interest today as pictorial reports of late eighteenth-century American life.

On repeated visits to New Milford, Earl was to paint no fewer than nineteen members of the Boardman family and their connections: the Taylors (Figure 26, 27, 35) and the Masterses. His picture of Jerusha Benedict (Figure 28), a visiting cousin from Danbury, is an exceptional example of his mastery of refined color harmony. He even turned out a likeness of the classic residence (Figure 37) Elijah Boardman had caused to be erected for his bride, completed in 1793 by the builder William Sprats. The house still stands on New Milford green. Earl admired Sprats-type houses and included several in other paintings.

The artist's itinerary led him from town to town, from village to village. In fashionable Litchfield were painted the engaging likenesses of the Seymours (Figures 21, 22, 23), the Tallmadges (Figure 29), and Mrs. John Watson (Figure 30); in Hartford, the daughters of Governor Wolcott, Mrs. Chauncy Goodrich and Mrs. William Moseley (Figure 31); in Sharon, Judge and Mrs. Judson Canfield, their three children, and a landscape complete with nine water birds and a house (Figure 36); in Fairfield, Mrs. Capers and the Burrs (Figure 38); in Windsor, Chief Justice and Mrs. Oliver Ellsworth (Figure 34) seated grandly before a window through which may be seen on a rise of ground an exterior view of the very house in which they are posing. *Looking East from Denny Hill* (Figure 41), perhaps the painter's most arresting example of pure landscape, was done at Worcester. So passed the closing decades of the 1700's; and so came picture by picture from Earl's loaded brush the faces of young America's people of quality, their children, and the possessions and scenes they loved. It is a record of high esthetic merit and major historic value.

What we know of the man himself during these years is meager indeed compared with the abundance of his output. His acceptability as a house guest is evidenced by his repeated returns to paint children and grandchildren at the homes of various clients. Despite the view that Earl usually wrote his own press notices, the exceptionally friendly tone of the following suggests that he may have had an anonymous admirer connected with the Litchfield *Weekly Monitor:*

Lichfield [*sic*]   May 18, 1796

Mr. *Ralph Earle,* the celebrated *Portrait Painter,* is now at New-Milford; where he will probably reside for some time. As we profess a friendship for Mr. *Earle,* and are desirous that the Public avail themselves of the abilities of this able artist, we feel a pleasure in making this communication; many gentlemen in this vicinity, having been disappointed of his services, and several of our friends being driven to accept of the paultry *daubs* of assuming pretenders. Mr. *Earle*'s price for a Portrait of full length is *Sixty Dollars*, the smaller size *Thirty Dollars*; the Painter finding his own support and materials.—Applications, by letter or otherwise, will be transmitted to Mr. *Earle* from this office, or the Post-master at New-Milford will take charge of all letters addressed to Mr. *Earle*.

If the so-called "self-portrait" (Figure 14) is indeed authentic, the painter made a pleasing appearance with his brown hair, gray-blue eye and sleek grooming. But what thoughts occupied that handsome head? Did he brood, one wonders, on his own forfeited status as he painted honored Revolutionary soldiers in uniform, well-heeled landowners, and popular political figures of the new order he had repudiated? Whatever the cause, a process of deterioration ultimately set in. With the passage of the years, he took increasingly to drink and became more and more careless about keeping engagements. His clientele began to dwindle. People who had hoped for his services turned to other artists whose work they admired less. A Mr. Whiting of New Hampshire, after contracting with Earl to paint his family, became at last so vexed by repeated postponements that he canceled the commission.

With the close of the century, Earl's art showed a sudden and shocking decline. His deft brushwork became clumsy; his lively draftsmanship turned inexpressibly crude. The ailing painter withdrew to quiet Bolton. Here, at the home of Dr. Samuel Cooley, a physician, Earl died in his fiftieth year on August 16, 1801. In the record of Bolton church, the pastor wrote "intemperance" as the cause. The location of his grave is unknown, though in all likelihood he lies in Bolton cemetery.

After death, Earl was forgotten. For over a century and a quarter his name was virtually unknown to students of American art. Stuart, Trumbull, Copley, and the Peales came in for their share of fame, but no honors fell to Earl. When in 1834, William Dunlap published his comprehensive chronicle of art in the United States,[22] he devoted scores of pages to himself and nearly as generous coverage to Stuart, Trumbull, and West. But Earl was dismissed with less than a page. Dunlap's neglect set a pattern for others, who continued to ignore Earl for generations. Some time in the 1930's, however, interest in him reawakened. The clean, literal honesty of his art has exceptional appeal for modern eyes. Today, hitherto unknown Earls are still being brought to light from unexpected places. Numbers of museums display his portraits proudly; one or two cherish rare landscapes.

The troubled genius who died so wretchedly at Bolton might well be surprised by the high and secure place his name now occupies on the roster of American painters. As if in belated apology for humiliations and neglect in the past, the present outdoes itself to reconstruct his career and proclaim his gifts. But Earl's most eloquent memorial is the gallery of paintings from his own inspired brush.

SELECTION OF REPRESENTATIVE
PAINTINGS

The pictures here reproduced are arranged in approximate chronological order according to actual and conjectural dates. Earl's first American period, which ended in 1778, is represented by one landscape and one portrait. The eleven specimens of his English period (1778-1785)—all portraits—show his rapid progression from naïve primitivism to his version of the more sophisticated elegance expected by sitters accustomed to pretentious portraiture. In his second American period (1785-1801), Earl's best years are judged to be from 1786 to about 1794, during which he produced canvas after canvas of outstanding excellence. Twenty pictures exemplify the work of this interval. Thereafter, his painting became increasingly uneven in quality until the painful deterioration of his closing days. That nearly to the last, however, the artist was capable of achievement of a high order is demonstrated by the seven works that conclude the series that follows.

FIGURE 2

ROGER SHERMAN

1721-1793

Though the aging statesman seems nearly as wooden as his Windsor chair, there is no mistaking the vigorous intelligence and stern integrity of the blue eyes, square jaw, and firm mouth. This portrait, produced by Earl in his mid-twenties, may well be his most penetrating psychological study. Even the hands—so often characterless and out of drawing in his later work—contribute to the suggestion of controlled power and rugged competence.

Roger Sherman was one of Connecticut's great citizens. A shoemaker before the Revolution, he studied surveying and law. He served in the General Assembly of Connecticut and became judge of the Supreme Court of the colony. He was a signer of the Declaration of Independence, the Articles of Confederation, and the Federal Constitution—having had a hand in drawing up the first and last. He represented his state in the first Congress.

Earl's color scheme is a low-keyed harmony of brown and black. The suit is deep rust; the hose, shoes, and chair legs, black. The subject sits alone in an empty corner where a sloping floor appears to tilt his chair forward at a curious angle. Though obviously the work of a provincial limner unfamiliar with more sophisticated paintings, the portrait communicates with a directness seldom achieved by the most accomplished artists.

Unsigned and undated
64⅝ x 49¾ inches
Yale University Art Gallery
New Haven, Connecticut
Gift of Roger Sherman White

FIGURE 3

A VIEW OF THE TOWN OF CONCORD

Because of his pictorial record of events at Lexington and Concord in 1775, Earl is generally accorded the distinction of being the first American painter of historical scenes.

The view of Concord has all the characteristics of a typical provincial landscape of the period. Painted shortly after the opening skirmishes of the Revolution, it shows British Redcoats in formation on the village common. Beyond them, citizens of the town—apparently all men—seem strolling sociably about as if unconcerned with the epochmaking incidents at hand.

The painting is spacious in concept and forthright in treatment. From the grassy elevation occupying the left foreground, one looks down upon cemetery and village green and out across a sweeping countryside of hills, trees, pond, and clustered houses.

Beside Doolittle's clumsy rendering of Pitcairn and Smith (Figure 1), the two officers in Earl's original are figures of some elegance. Though strangely proportioned, they have distinction of bearing. The uniform coats are tomato red, pink lined, and trimmed with gold braid. Each man wears yellow breeches, yellow waistcoat, and a red sash. Boots and tricorns are black, the latter edged with gold.

Of the four paintings constituting Earl's Lexington-Concord series, this is the only one so far discovered.

Unsigned and undated
29½ x 38½ inches
Mrs. Stedman Buttrick, Sr.
Concord, Massachusetts

17

FIGURE 4

WILLIAM CARPENTER
1767-1823

William's portrait is one of a pair of the earliest English Earls so far to come to light. The other is a likeness of his sister Mary Ann. His father was William Carpenter, Gentleman, of Aldeby Priory, Norfolk. The sitter spent his adult life at Toft Monks, some two miles from his childhood home. His name is inscribed on a white marble slab among other Carpenter memorial tablets placed by his seven sons on the walls of the little country church at Aldeby.

The fair-haired twelve-year-old in his scarlet suit is portrayed with literal simplicity. His face, though agreeable, has a mask-like immobility. The stool tilts at the same angle as Sherman's chair (Figure 2), its legs casting long parallel shadows. The hinge of the folding table, the very grain of the wood, are depicted with photographic realism. Yet there is much unnatural distortion.

Compared with the informed urbanity Earl was soon to achieve from exposure to the great English portraitists, this work displays the gaucherie of folk art. Yet this very quality, retained to the end of his days, adds peculiar charm to his most characteristic pictures. It comes close to disappearing in such canvases as *Sophia Drake* (Figure 10) and *Unidentified Doctor of Divinity* (Figure 12), but survives the artist's English period to lend stylistic distinction to his numerous American paintings.

Signed and dated 1779
47⅞ x 35⅝ inches
Worcester Art Museum
Worcester, Massachusetts

Figure 5

COLONEL GEORGE ONSLOW, M.P.
1731-1792

On May 1, 1783, *The Morning Post, and Daily Advertiser* (London) included the following paragraph among its comments on "the principal Pictures, Busts, Drawings, &c. now exhibiting at the Royal Academy":

R. EARL.

No. 65—A most excellent likeness of George Onslow, Esq., in shooting dress, playing with a spaniel. There are parts of the drapery remarkably well cast.

This work was the first of four portraits of men entered by Earl in Royal Academy exhibitions between 1783 and 1785.

Colonel George Onslow, Member of Parliament from Guildford, out-ranger of Windsor forest, and master of Desborough House at Ripley, Surrey, here appears in red-and-white striped waistcoat, brown coat, and corded buff breeches. These constitute the well-cast "drapery." The dog looks like a pointer to present-day viewers, but in eighteenth-century parlance would have passed as a "smooth spaniel."[23] The fowling piece is an exact likeness of one of the Colonel's still extant.

Both painting and gun remained the property of Onslow's descendants in Ripley until recently brought to the United States.

Unsigned and undated
52 x 42 inches
Ralph Earle
Haverford, Pennsylvania

FIGURE 6

SOPHIA ISHAM
1772-1851

When painted by Earl, Sophia Isham, aged eleven years, was a pupil at the school for young ladies kept by the Misses Dutton at Windsor, England. In December, 1783, her father, Sir Justinian Isham, seventh baronet, of Lamport Hall, Northampton, received a bill from the school which listed among other items, "To Miss Sophia's portrait—£5:5:0."[24]

In keeping with the tender grace of its subject, the portrait is rendered in fresh colors applied with lightness and delicacy. In a shimmering gown of lettuce-green trimmed with pale pink ruching, the girl stands against a background of foliage and river scenery, presumably along the Thames. The distant white church spire shows Earl's early partiality for a feature that became a kind of signature in his later American paintings.

At the age of twenty-one, Miss Isham married Thomas Palmer, eldest son of Sir John Palmer, fifth baronet, of Carlon, Northampton. Her portrait, however, remained at Lamport Hall, where it hangs in the dining room today.

Signed and dated 1783
38½ x 28 inches
Sir Gyles Isham, Bart.
Lamport, Northampton, England

FIGURE 7

REAR ADMIRAL RICHARD KEMPENFELT
1718-1782

The naval hero stands on the seashore, his right elbow propped on the fluke of an anchor. He wears the correct dress uniform of a flag officer and carries a telescope. The man-of-war in the offing may be one of the ships Kempenfelt commanded, although the blue flag at the main mast signifies an admiral, a rank he never held.

The date, which can be seen with the artist's signature along the arm of the anchor, may be read either 1782 or 1783. Kempenfelt went down with the *Royal George* at Spithead on August 29, 1782. Though his portrait could have been begun before his death, it seems certain that most of it was done thereafter. The improper display of the flag would surely have been corrected had he lived to see the finished picture.

Moreover, Earl borrowed the general plan of this work from a variety of sources, a procedure to which the living model might have raised objections. The arrangement of the arms, hand, and telescope is obviously derived from Gainsborough's painting of Augustus John, third Earl of Bristol, who, like Kempenfelt, leans on an anchor. The ship combines features from two other pictures. Altogether, it appears that the young artist, commissioned to produce a likeness of the drowned naval officer, relied extensively on such existing representations of a nautical character as he could readily find.

Signed and dated 1782 or 1783
50 x 39 inches
National Portrait Gallery
London

FIGURE 8

A MASTER IN CHANCERY ENTERING THE HOUSE OF LORDS

While the identity of the subject has not been established beyond question, research[25] indicates that it is probably Henry, second Earl of Bathurst (1714-1794), son of Allen, first Earl, who served as treasurer to George, Prince of Wales, later George III. Henry became Chief Justice of the Common Pleas in 1754 and Lord Chancellor in 1771, with the title Baron Apsley. He resigned in 1778.

Shown against a background presumed to represent a parliamentary chamber, the ex-Lord Chancellor wears the black suit and black silk robe of the high courts of England. Wig, bands, and frilled cuffs are white. The scroll under his left arm bears the following in script: "An Act to restrain / Trade of Massach / Rhodeisland Con / Virginia South Ca / North America." According to Parks[26] these fragments pertain to two bills written by Lord North, the Prime Minister of England, that were passed and repealed in 1775. They were designed to restrain trade with the northern and southern colonies respectively.

Earl entered *A Master in Chancery* in the Royal Academy exhibit of May, 1784.

Signed and dated 1783
49¼ x 39 inches
Smith College Museum of Art
Northampton, Massachusetts

26

Figure 9

MARIANNE DRAKE
1764-1849

The elder of the Drake sisters was evidently adept in accomplishments considered appropriate for a young eighteenth-century lady of fashion. Paint brush in hand, she sits with her box of colors at her elbow and a two-manual harpsichord of baroque design behind her. The play of light on the lustrous white satin gown and pink sash is conveyed by sure, slashing brushwork.

The watercolor held up for our approval shows the typical white church spire by a narrow stream or canal not much wider than the masted barge floating by just above the holder's thumb. Because of the resemblance of this scene to that behind Sophia Isham, it has been suggested that the Drake sisters might have been her schoolmates at Windsor. Drake family records[26] indicate, however that both Marianne and Sophia went to school in London.

In 1792, Marianne married Thomas Evance of Lambeth, recorder of the borough of Kingston. After his death in 1830, she presented his half-length portrait to the Kingston Town Hall, where it still hangs in the Council Chamber. Her second husband was John McIntosh.

Signed and dated 1783
c. 50 x 40 inches
Count Charles de Salis
Bondo, Switzerland

FIGURE 10

SOPHIA DRAKE
1765-1803

The Drake sisters were the only children of Admiral Francis William Drake, a great-great-great-grandson of Thomas, the brother of the famous Sir Francis Drake of Elizabethan times. They lived at Hillingdon Place, Middlesex, a substantial property situated near that of Jerome de Salis, Count of the Holy Roman Empire, Deputy Lieutenant for Middlesex and Armagh, and Knight of the Golden Spur. Sophia married Jerome in 1797.

Earl's picture of the future countess is exceptionally pleasing in composition, the line of the tree completing and complimenting the graceful positioning of the figure. The summery dress of cross-barred muslin and sash of French blue silk tied at the back are depicted with the artist's usual deftness in representing fabrics. Matching blue ribbons trim the large hat of Leghorn straw.

Hillingdon Place and its furnishings were inherited by Sophia, including Earl's portraits of herself and Marianne. The two pictures hung in the dining room of the mansion as late as 1875. Soon thereafter, the grandfather of the present Count conveyed them to Bondo, Switzerland, where they are now to be seen on the staircase of the family palazzo, a stately eighteenth-century residence that commands one of the important Alpine passes.

Signed and dated 1784
c. 50 x 40 inches
Count Charles de Salis
Bondo, Switzerland

FIGURE 11

HUNTER WITH GUN AND DOGS

The unidentified English gentleman in red coat and buff breeches stands as if in a stage spotlight against a somber backdrop scene of overcast sky and trees that throw horizontal shadows across a level lawn. In one hand he holds a fowling piece and in the other a black hat lined with blue.

The work is structurally sound and strikingly decorative. While the hunter has an air of gracious charm, his body appears unnaturally elongated and seems to dwindle above the waist. The narrow shoulders and slender arms are a shade too slight for the substantial legs. Throughout his painting career, Earl occasionally turned out a full length standing male figure exhibiting these characteristics.

As for the boots, should the modern viewer conclude that this nimrod wears two right ones, he is reminded that in the eighteenth century both the left and the right shoes were commonly made on the same last. The shoemaker carved a single wooden form approximating the size and shape of his customer's feet and thereon molded both shoes of a pair. They were essentially identical.

Signed *Earle* and dated 1784
86⅛ x 57½ inches
Worcester Art Museum
Worcester, Massachusetts

FIGURE 12

UNIDENTIFIED DOCTOR OF DIVINITY

This late product of Earl's English period, when compared with his portrait of William Carpenter (Figure 4), shows dramatically how far the artist had gone in five years toward losing the wooden primitivism conspicuous in his earlier efforts. The humorous face seems alive and mobile rather than masklike. The robes fall richly and gracefully as Reynolds might have disposed them. The hands have relaxed naturalness.

The picture is composed with a sure sense of design. Focus on the fine head is achieved by lighting, lines of the vestments, the very angles of the books to the right. By any standards, this is a sophisticated work.

The robes are apparently those of an Oxford doctor of divinity. On the spines of the books, the names of Gay and Locke are discernible.

Signed and dated 1784
Present whereabouts unknown

FIGURE 13

ANN WHITESIDE (MRS. RALPH EARL)
c. 1762-1826

The provenance of this picture is obscure prior to 1913, when, entitled *Wife of the Artist*, it was put up for sale in London by an unnamed owner. Nevertheless, considerable confidence is felt in identifying the sitter as Ann, daughter of Eleazer Whiteside of Norwich, Norfolk, whom Earl was to take back to Massachusetts as his wife the year after completion of this portrait.

Her lover has portrayed her with exceptional appreciation of character. Revealed is a person of reserve and gentle grace with heartshaped face, delicate complexion, clear hazel eyes, and curling hair. Over the white blouse of cross-barred muslin and the lustrous skirt of white silk, she wears a black, lace-edged shawl that covers her shoulders and loops softly about her arms. The sash is pale yellow. In her hands is a partially rolled map, and behind her stands a large terrestrial globe so turned as to show the west coast of North America. The olive-green curtain is drawn back to discover shelves of books.

Signed and dated 1784
46⅝ x 37⅞ inches
Amherst College
Amherst, Massachusetts

FIGURE 14

RALPH EARL
1751-1801

Although there exist grave doubts in some quarters as to this portrait's being either of or by Ralph Earl, William Sawitzky, the late Earl scholar, had sufficient confidence in its authenticity to include it in the Connecticut Tercentenary exhibition of the artist's paintings at Yale in 1935.[28] It was omitted, however, from the check list of Earl's English paintings in the *Worcester Art Museum Annual* for 1960.[29]

If, as appears, the subject's age is here about thirty, the picture represents Earl's English period. Perhaps it was done at the request of the second Mrs. Earl, as Rathbone[30] suggests—possibly about the time her own likeness was painted.

The rather self-conscious rigidity of the sitter's pose is natural for a person whose attention is divided between his reflection in a mirror and the self-likeness taking shape on the drawing board before him. The eyes are gray-blue, the hair brown. Coat and waistcoat are light green, while the brocaded chair back is crimson.

Unsigned and undated
30 x 25¼ inches
City Art Museum of St. Louis, Missouri

FIGURE 15

AMOS DOOLITTLE
1754-1832

Despite the brick-red table cover and the white waistcoat, this is a somber picture. The outline of the head is almost lost against the deep green curtain. The coat is dark brown. Dimly-seen bookshelves and stretch of blank wall combine with dusky foreground to produce a shut-in effect.

The sitter is identified by his signature on the rolled sheet lying before him. It is interesting to have this likeness of the friend with whom Earl explored the sites of the battles of Lexington and Concord and who later produced the copper engravings of the artist's paintings of these scenes (Figures 1 and 3). His is a distinguished face—eyes handsome under arched brows, nose well formed, lips sensitively modeled. There is about it, however, an air of brooding taciturnity as it looks out from its shadowy surroundings.

Although the portrait was at one time considered a work of Earl's pre-English period, it is now assumed to have been painted shortly after the artist's return to America.

Unsigned and undated
36 x 28 inches
Lyman Allyn Museum
New London, Connecticut

FIGURE 16

THOMAS EARLE
1737-1819

While no one questions this portrait's being by Earl, a cousin of the sitter, it is generally agreed that the signature and date (1800) were added by a later hand. Stylistically, the work suggests an earlier phase of the artist's development. Considered by some to be a product of the first American period, it seems to others to belong to the mid-1780's.

Thomas Earle, a man of considerable mechanical ability, made guns for the Americans during the Revolutionary war. There is a story[31] of his going afoot to New York City to deliver a gun of his making to General Washington.

A detailed view of his house and shops in Cherry Valley, Massachusetts, is seen through the window. On the day of the battle of Lexington, the owner is reported to have planted five rows of sycamores in front of his home. Behind it rises Bald Hill.

37½ x 34 inches
The National Gallery of Art
Washington, D.C.
Mellon Collection

FIGURE 17

GENTLEMAN WITH NEGRO ATTENDANT

This interesting work, though somewhat cramped in composition, is exceptionally colorful. Seated in a chair tapestried in dull rose, the unidentified gentleman wears a dark green coat partially open to show the richly embroidered waistcoat with double row of gold buttons and gold piping. The background is divided to set off the two heads—dark brown behind the gentleman with his powdered wig, light gray behind the boy, who wears a tomato-red jacket and white collar. The latter is one of the earliest Negro portraits in American art.

Although Earl, not infrequently, identified sitters by inscriptions on letters shown in pictures, no name appears on the note being delivered in this painting. There could so easily have been one.

It is judged that this picture was painted between 1785 and 1790.

Unsigned and undated
30 x 25 inches
New Britain Museum of American Art
New Britain, Rhode Island

FIGURE 18

MAJOR GENERAL FREDERICK WILLIAM AUGUSTUS, BARON VON STEUBEN
1730-1794

Of Prussian descent, Baron von Steuben served in the army of Frederick the Great before coming to this country in 1777. His offer of assistance to the American cause having been accepted by Congress, he proved so effective a drill master and counselor on strategic warfare that the relatively undisciplined American army was rapidly converted into a military force to be reckoned with. Washington considered his contribution to the success of the Revolution one that could have been provided by no one else. Congress showed its gratitude by presenting him with a dress sword, the silver hilt of which is seen in Earl's painting.

Steuben wears the blue and yellow uniform of the Continental Army. The star of the Prussian Order of Fidelity hangs around his neck, and its badge decorates his breast. On the lapel are the insignia of the American Society of the Cincinnati, of which he was a founder. An expanse of blue water lies to his right, on the shore of which stand white tents of an encampment.

The Baron became an American citizen and was a much-admired friend of the Alexander Hamiltons, with whom he stayed while his host was trying to get a pension for him from the government.

This portrait was given by the subject to James Duane, first mayor of New York City. A near replica, unsigned and undated, hangs in the Yale University Art Gallery.

Signed and dated 1786
48½ x 40 inches
New York State Historical Association
Cooperstown, New York

FIGURE 19

MRS. ALEXANDER HAMILTON
1757-1854

One would never guess that this queenly portrait of one of America's most aristocratic ladies was painted within prison walls where the artist was confined for debt. Dressed in white, hair curled and powdered, the occupant of the blue and gold chair must have seemed a strange caller at the old New York bridewell. In any case, the likeness is of exceptional vitality and charm, the only known portrait made of its subject before the tragic death of her husband.

Daughter of Major Philip Schuyler and Catherine Van Rensselaer, Elizabeth Schuyler in 1780 married Alexander Hamilton, then still a young officer on Washington's staff. Staunchly loyal to her husband, Mrs. Hamilton devoted the forty-eight years of her widowhood to protecting and promoting his renown.

Signed and dated 1787
32½ x 27½ inches
Museum of the City of New York

FIGURE 20

GENERAL MATTHEW CLARKSON
1758-1825

Descended from generations of old New York families of established social position, Matthew Clarkson, at the age of seventeen, joined the Army of the Revolution. He served at the outset as aide-de-camp to General Benedict Arnold and later in like capacity to General Benjamin Lincoln. During his distinguished military career, he participated in two of the greatest American reverses—the defeat on Long Island and the fall of Charleston—and in two of the most brilliant American successes—the surrender of General Burgoyne at Saratoga and that of Lord Cornwallis at Yorktown.

When painted by Earl, he was a widower of twenty-nine. He had but recently returned from a mission in France for the University of the State of New York, where he was presented at the court of Louis XVI. The date of this portrait and the sitter's close friendship with the Alexander Hamiltons make it probable that Clarkson was among the persons of fashion who posed for Earl in the New York city jail at the time of the artist's imprisonment. For the sittings, he wore a dark blue coat, striped buff vest, and white stock.

After the Revolution, Clarkson became a leader in politics and movements for public improvement. He was an early member of the Cincinnati, a regent of the University of the State of New York, member of the Assembly, United States marshall, member of the State Senate for two terms, president of the New York Hospital, and president of the Bank of New York. Always the champion of human freedom, he introduced the Assembly bill for gradual abolition of slavery in New York, and never missed an opportunity to defend the rights of the Negro.

Signed and dated 1787
27 x 21¾ inches
Gilcrease Institute
Tulsa, Oklahoma

FIGURE 21

MAJOR MOSES SEYMOUR
1742-1826

Contemporary comments on the Moses Seymours of Litchfield, Connecticut, indicate that theirs was a happy household. Earl's four likenesses of the family show a handsome, intelligent, and humorous set of faces.

Major Seymour, a well-to-do merchant before the Revolution, served during much of the conflict as commissary of supplies at Litchfield, which was a supply depot for the American forces and a detention center for prisoners of war. Nevertheless, he commanded a troop of cavalry in the battles of Long Island, Bemis Heights, Stillwater, and Saratoga, and participated in the Tryon raids on Danbury, Ridgefield, and New Haven. Following the war, he held the office of town clerk of Litchfield for thirty-seven years and represented the town for sixteen years in the state legislature. To the last of his days, he wore the queue, small clothes, shoe buckles, and white-top boots of eighteenth-century fashion.

His portrait shows him in the blue and buff uniform of the Connecticut militia—sword in one hand, cockaded tricorn in the other, a red shoulder sash. He stands in pleasant rural surroundings on the outskirts of Litchfield, the white church spire of which pierces the skyline in the distance.

Signed and dated 1789
48 x 35⅞ inches
City Art Museum of St. Louis, Missouri

FIGURE 22

MRS. MOSES SEYMOUR AND SON EPAPHRODITUS
1752-1826   1783-1853

Molly Marsh, daughter of Colonel Ebenezer Marsh, married Moses Seymour in 1771. Epaphroditus, youngest of their six children, was in later life president of the bank in Brattleboro, Vermont.

The picture is noteworthy for character insight and warm color harmony. Mother and son, so similar in features, seem to share a twinkling good humor and relaxed self-possession. Tones of rust and gold predominate, with white distributed through the composition to lighten the total effect.

In his comments on this work, Perry T. Rathbone[32] quotes an illuminating contemporary reference to the Seymours.

> Thanks to a distinguished prisoner, David Matthews, the loyalist Mayor of New York, who was confined to the Seymour's home during the Revolution, we have an appraisal of Molly Seymour's character. In a letter to his wife, Matthews wrote, "Ever since my arrival here, I have been at the house of Captain Moses Seymour, who together with his wife have behaved in the most genteel, kind manner and have done everything in their power to make my time as agreeable as possible. They have nothing of the Yankee about them. He is a fine merry fellow, and she is a warm protestant, and if it were not that the thoughts of home were constantly in my mind, I might be happy with my good landlord and his family to whom I wish you could send some tea, if it were possible, as there is none to be bought here."

Signed and dated 1789
48 x 36 inches
City Art Museum of St. Louis, Missouri

FIGURE 23

CLARISSA SEYMOUR
1772-1865

Clarissa Seymour, here seventeen, was the daughter of Major Moses and Molly (Marsh) Seymour. The Reverend Truman Marsh, whom she married in 1791, was a Yale graduate and for twenty-three years minister of St. Michael's Episcopal Church at Litchfield.

The sitter's bright, friendly face is highlighted against the somber foliage of the nearer trees. Her billowy dress is of rose-colored material with white muslin overskirt and fringed sash. She holds a folded fan. Through the vista of trees is seen a wooded point of land at the bend of a river—a landscape feature evidently pleasing to Earl, for he used it repeatedly in the pictures of both his English and second American periods.

Signed and dated 1789
48½ x 36½ inches
The Brooklyn Museum, New York

FIGURE 24

MAJOR DANIEL BOARDMAN
1757-1833

The elegant young Federalist merchant shares the canvas with one of the most delightful of Earl's landscape backgrounds. The result is a dual portrait of a person and a place. Between the winding Housatonic and distant wooded hills, New Milford, Connecticut, lifts its chimneys and church spire into the fading sunset light.

A grandson of the Reverend Daniel Boardman, first minister of the church that dominates the view, the subject, born in New Milford, was conducting a dry-goods business there with his brother Elijah at the time the portrait was painted. Having helped his father with the family farm until the age of nineteen, he was placed for instruction in 1776 with his uncle, the Reverend Daniel Ferrand of Canaan, Connecticut, who prepared him for entering Yale in the fall of the following year. Here he received both the A.B. and M.A. degrees. Chosen captain of a military company established in New Milford, he was later appointed major of the regiment to which it was attached. He twice represented New Milford in the General Assembly. In 1795 he moved to New York City, where he engaged in a wholesale mercantile business. He married Hetty Moore of New York in 1797.

Wearing a dark blue coat, white double-breasted waistcoat trimmed in gold braid, white knee breeches, and clocked stockings, Major Boardman here seems the prototype of the fashionable eighteenth-century American gentleman of means. The ivory-headed walking stick on which he leans is today a cherished possession of one of his descendants.

Signed and dated 1789
81⅝ x 55¼ inches
The National Gallery of Art
Washington, D.C.
Gift of Mrs. W. Murray Crane

FIGURE 25

ELIJAH BOARDMAN
1760-1823

Just as his brother Daniel steps aside to permit the observer a view of his native town, here Elijah allows a fascinating glimpse into the dry-goods store which the two brothers operated in New Milford, Connecticut. The tall, aristocratic figure stands in arresting contrast to the mercantile setting. With one frilled wrist resting on his desk, the dapper draper poses in faun coat with gold buttons on cuffs, black breeches, white clocked hose, and black buckled slippers. Books on the shelves—which include Moore's *Travels,* Shakespeare, *Paradise Lost*, Johnson's dictionary, and the *London Magazine* for 1787—give some clue to the owner's intellectual interests.

That the store provided a fair choice of merchandise may be judged from the array of yard goods seen through the open door. The village shopper intent on a new dress might here select materials from bolts of white, pale pink, pale blue, coral, brown with yellow spots, taupe, light green, pale lavender, white with brown and yellow stripes, white sprigged with red and brown, pale yellow, and gray.

Elijah Boardman was a soldier and statesman as well as business man. In 1776, aged sixteen, he enlisted in the army, serving in regiments of the Connecticut line. As a merchant, he carried his activities into the Connecticut lands in Ohio, where he founded the town of Boardman. In 1792, he married Mary Ann Whiting, for whom he built the Boardman house still standing on New Milford green (Figure 37). Elected six times to the state legislature, first as representative and later as senator, he was United States Senator from 1821 until his death, which occurred during a family visit in Boardman, Ohio.

Signed and dated 1789
83 x 51 inches
Mrs. Cornelius Boardman Tyler
Fairfield, New Jersey

FIGURE 26

COLONEL WILLIAM TAYLOR
1764-1841

Earl's mastery of color and composition is apparent in this representation of the young Yale graduate, who evidently had a flare for fashion as well as military achievement. The long gray-brown coat, the vest striped in green and white, and the green upholstery of the roundabout chair produce an arresting color pattern. The vigorous but slightly theatrical pose of the sitter shows the lingering influence on Earl of his contact with the grand manner of English portraiture.

Son of the Reverend Nathanael and Tamar (Boardman) Taylor, the Colonel built and occupied in 1784 the house beside his father's church that still overlooks the New Milford green. In 1786, he married Abigail Starr of Danbury. He was appointed captain of the 8th Regiment Cavalry in 1791, major in 1796, and lieutenant-colonel in 1802.

Signed and dated 1790
48½ x 38 inches
Albright-Knox Art Gallery
Buffalo, New York
Charles Clifton Fund

FIGURE 27

THE REVEREND NATHANAEL TAYLOR
1722-1800

Having been graduated from Yale in 1745 and licensed to preach in 1747, Nathanael Taylor, born in Danbury, came to New Milford in 1748 and the next year married the daughter of the Reverend Daniel Boardman, whom he succeeded as Congregational minister, a post in which he served for fifty-two years.

Considered a great athlete while in college, he is declared by one chronicler[33] to be the only person who ever kicked a football over a Yale college building. A member of the board of trustees of Yale for twenty-six years, he managed the college farms as well. He also maintained a grammar school. Ardently supporting the Revolution, he served as chaplain to a regiment of Connecticut troops and during the struggle remitted a year's salary to help relieve the financial burden of his parish.

The pastor is represented in his pulpit. The small Bible is said to have been a gift from his father. This he always held in his hand while preaching, having placed therein a copy of his sermon written in small hand on sheets of paper of a size to lie unobserved between the pages.

The conjectural date of the painting is 1790, one of Earl's busy years in New Milford.

Unsigned and undated
48 x 37 inches
Addison Gallery of American Art
Phillips Academy
Andover, Massachusetts

FIGURE 28

JERUSHA BENEDICT
1772-1795

The brown-eyed subject was five years old when her father's house in Danbury, Connecticut, was burned by the British. Daughter of Zadock Benedict, founder of the Danbury hat industry, she became in 1792 the wife of Isaac Ives—Yale graduate, lawyer, and deacon of the First Congregational Church of Danbury. She died while they were visiting his parents in Meriden, where she is buried. Their home, the old Ives homestead, still stands in Danbury.

Since there is no evidence that Earl painted in Danbury, it is assumed that this portrait was done during one of the sitter's visits to her Taylor cousins in New Milford. The artist's likeness of Colonel William Taylor (Figure 26) is dated 1790 and that of Reverend Nathanael Taylor (Figure 27), though undated, is assigned to the same year. The church spire in the distance has the corner pinnacles that distinguished the original New Milford steeple, as can be seen in the portrait of Major Daniel Boardman (Figure 24), another cousin of Miss Benedict's.

This painting is noteworthy among Earls for refined color harmony. The soft woodrose of the taffeta with its silvery highlights, the rich brownish-red of the table, and the bronzy autumn shades of the background foliage are combined to produce an over-all warmth of tone. Touches of impasto accent embroidery designs on frills and fichu and bring out the texture of the black and white plumes of the headdress. To the right, beyond a stream's bend typical of Earl, lie sunlit fields set off by minute rail fences.

Signed and dated 1790
38 x 31¾ inches
Private collection

FIGURE 29

MRS. BENJAMIN TALLMADGE WITH SON AND DAUGHTER
1763-1805   1787-?   1790-1878

Mrs. Tallmadge, born Mary Floyd, was the daughter of William Floyd, a signer of the Declaration of Independence. In 1784, she married Colonel Benjamin Tallmadge (1754-1855), a Yale graduate who gained a reputation for resourcefulness and daring during the Revolution, served sixteen years in Congress, and became president of a Litchfield bank. Of their five children, Henry Floyd is here shown seated on the floor and Maria Jones on her mother's lap.

Says Saint-Gaudins of this group portrait, "There is character in every rigid detail right up to the fascinating headdress."[34] The sitters are without suggestion of affected graces. For all her elegant attire, the mother looks directly into the eyes of the spectator with honesty and self-respecting composure. Though one of the dressiest of Earl's works, there is nothing fancy about his representation. He simply depicts with straightforward fidelity every pleat and ruffle of the blue satin gown; the fine lace of the fichu; the decorations of the fan; the pearls, plumes, and flowers of the coiffure. One cannot doubt that this finery was the height of American fashion in 1790, though in some respects it would have been considered behind the times in France and England. Style changes traveled slowly in the eighteenth century.

Henry, like all very small boys of the time, wears a dress that seems to modern viewers more appropriate for a girl. Earl often demonstrates small aptitude for portraying little children, his likenesses of the young Tallmadges being typical of his usual showing in this respect. The miniature toy coach is a delightful inclusion. As in many of Earl's American portraits, the intricately patterned Axminister carpet lends depth and suggests a well-furnished room.

Signed and dated 1790
78 x 54 inches
Litchfield Historical Society
Litchfield, Connecticut

FIGURE 30

MRS. JOHN WATSON
1708-1792

The likeness of Mrs. John Watson has been pronounced "one of the most appealing character studies of an elderly person in all early American portraiture."[35]

The eighty-four-year-old subject, spectacles in hand, seems on the point of reading her Bible, which is open to I. Kings. The trim erectness of her alert figure is accented by the strongly defined window frame and the column at the right. Through the window are seen Bantam Lake and the distant white spire of the church in Litchfield, Connecticut.

Mrs. Watson, born Bethia Tyler in Wallingford, Connecticut, married in 1730 and later lived in Litchfield. She was the great-grandmother of James Watson Williams, whose daughters left money to found Munson-Williams-Proctor Institute, where the portrait now hangs.

The artist's signature and the date extend along the baseboard at the left, between and on both sides of the table legs. As with a number of Earls of this size, the canvas is pieced. In this case the seam runs vertically through the sitter's right knee and forearm and thence invisibly up the window frame.

Signed and dated 1791
58 x 54 inches
Munson-Williams-Proctor Institute
Utica, New York

FIGURE 31

MRS. WILLIAM MOSELEY AND SON CHARLES
1761-1814   1786/7-1815

Writing to her brother from Hartford, Connecticut, on September 28, 1791, Laura Moseley reported that her "attention had been engrossed by Mr. Earl," a preoccupation that was developing in her "the grace of patience," in which she would probably "arrive at a state of perfection" in the course of two or three months. Remarks that the "painting goes on steadily though slowly" and that the artist "has two or three others on hand" shed light on Earl's work ways.[36]

Mrs. Moseley was the daughter of Oliver Wolcott of Litchfield, a signer of the Declaration of Independence and later governor of Connecticut. Her brother Oliver, Jr., became governor also. In 1785, she married William Moseley, a Hartford lawyer. Their only child, Charles, after graduating from Yale, also practiced law in Hartford.

Aged three or four years in this picture, Charles looks exceptionally mature in both face and figure. Gray-eyed and yellow-haired, he wears a red suit with brass buttons. His mother's coat, dark blue trimmed with gold braid and brass buttons, is worn over a white dress. The spectacular hat is white. She carries black gloves.

Looking beyond blue water and rolling green fields, one sees on the skyline the steeples of a distant town. This presumably is Hartford, where the Moseleys lived and where this picture was painted.

Signed and dated 1791
86¾ x 68¼ inches
Yale University Art Gallery
New Haven, Connecticut
Bequest of Mrs. Katherine Rankin
Wolcott Verplanck

FIGURE 32

COLONEL SAMUEL TALCOTT
1711-1797

Son of Joseph Talcott, colonial governor of Connecticut, Samuel graduated from Yale College in 1733. In 1739, he married Mabel Wyllys, great-granddaughter of Governor George Wyllys. He had no need to follow a profession, having inherited a large estate from his father. During the Revolution, he commanded a regiment raised to go against Crown Point. Later, he represented Hartford in the General Assembly.

His life was that of a gentleman of taste and means. Highly regarded as a leading citizen of Hartford, in 1770 he built a large house, the interior of which was famous for its fine cabinet work. His time was devoted largely to public affairs and management of his extensive property.

Earl portrayed the octogenarian seated in his library, one hand resting on a sheet of paper bearing three lines of indecipherable writing. His dark suit is blue green, his chair red. The handsome face, though austere, is one to inspire trust. Talcott's is considered one of the artist's finest heads.

Beyond the neat little fences and trees seen through the window, one catches a distant glimpse of the church spires of Hartford.

The presumed date of the painting is 1791.

Unsigned and undated
71¼ x 53¾ inches
Wadsworth Atheneum
Hartford, Connecticut

FIGURE 33

COLONEL MARINUS WILLETT
1740-1830

Girt with the sword presented him by Congress, the fair-haired, blue-eyed colonel strikes a grandiose attitude reminscent of *Hunter with Gun and Dogs* (Figure 11), painted by Earl in England a decade earlier. He wears the deep-blue and white uniform of the New York militia, silver epaulets, and the eagle badge of the American Society of the Cincinnati. Apprehensive redskins in the offing recall the patriot's prowess as an Indian fighter.

Willett was born in Jamaica, L.I., and began his military career in the French and Indian War. Before the Revolution, he was a cabinetmaker in New York. Active throughout the Revolution, he was with Washington in New Jersey in 1778, accompanied General Sullivan against the Iroquois in 1779, and was later commissioned to negotiate treaties with the Creeks. At one time sheriff of New York County, he succeeded De Witt Clinton as mayor of New York City in 1807. He died at his farm near Corlear's Hook.

The conjectural date is 1791.

Unsigned and undated
91¼ x 56 inches
The Metropolitan Museum of Art
New York
Bequest of George Willett Van Nest
1917

77

FIGURE 34

CHIEF JUSTICE AND MRS. OLIVER ELLSWORTH
1745-1807   1756-1818

The Ellsworths are represented in the "Washington room" of their home, so-called because it was here that General Washington sat when he visited them at Windsor, Connecticut. Beyond the open window is a view of Elmwood, the very house in which they sit. Built in 1740 on the west bank of the Connecticut river, its ell was added by Ellsworth in 1783. Around it he planted thirteen elms, one for each of the original states.[37]

Oliver Ellsworth attended both Yale and Princeton, receiving the A.B. from the latter in 1766. He was one of the most distinguished figures of the Revolution and served the government in important posts both at home and abroad. In 1777, he was elected a delegate to the Continental Congress. He represented Connecticut at the Federal Convention at Philadelphia in 1787. One of the committee of five that drew up the first official draft of the United States Constitution, he is shown with a copy of it in his hand. United States Senator from Connecticut from 1788 to 1796, he later served as Chief Justice of the United States Supreme Court from 1796 to 1801. An outstanding lawyer, he was awarded the LL.D. on three different occasions— by Yale, Dartmouth, and Princeton. He was much interested in agriculture, to which he devoted his attention when he retired in 1801. He died at Elmwood six years later.

His wife was Abigail Wolcott of East Windsor, whom he married in 1772.

The Ellsworth homestead still stands, maintained by the local chapter of the Daughters of the American Revolution.

Signed and dated 1792
76 x 85 inches
Wadsworth Atheneum
Hartford, Connecticut
Gift of the Ellsworth
Heirs

FIGURE 35

CHILDREN OF COLONEL NATHANIEL TAYLOR

John, Charlotte, and Nathaniel William Taylor were grandchildren of the Reverend Nathaniel Taylor (Figure 27) of New Milford. When painted, they were respectively nineteen, fourteen, and ten years of age. Their father, a Revolutionary officer, was an apothecary and druggist in that village; their mother the former Anna Northrup.

Charlotte's yellow dress stands out in luminous contrast to the black suits of her brothers. She has pink roses around her neck and on her head. The sash is blue and the pearls at her throat are strung on a red cord.

This has been pronounced one of the finest pictures of children done by Earl,[38] whose likenesses of youngsters tend to be somewhat grim and unnaturally mature. The drawing of Charlotte's hands betrays a recurring carelessness or inaptitude in depicting these members that begins to become more noticeable in Earl's pictures about this time.

Signed and dated 1796
48 x 48½ inches
Private collection

FIGURE 36

LANDSCAPE PAINTED NEAR SHARON

In 1796, while painting the portraits of Judge Judson Canfield, his wife, and children, Earl was a house guest at their home near Sharon, Connecticut. According to family tradition, he felt indebted to them for their hospitality and painted this landscape as a present to the judge at the time of his departure.

While the house may represent the Canfield mansion—now gone—the scene is presumed imaginary. It is, on the whole, a somber view—dull blue water, dark green trees, a faded sky faintly flushed with rose. The buildings are dwarfed by the disproportionately large trees. Groups of waterbirds are seen in the foreground and beyond the arched bridge of improbable design. A charming litle inn, with swinging sign and empty carriage shed, stands where the two roads meet. The innkeeper at the door is the only human being astir in the strangely deserted countryside.

Unsigned and undated
34⅝ x 72½ inches
Litchfield Historical Society
Litchfield, Connecticut
Bequest of Mrs. Edward W. Seymour, 1917

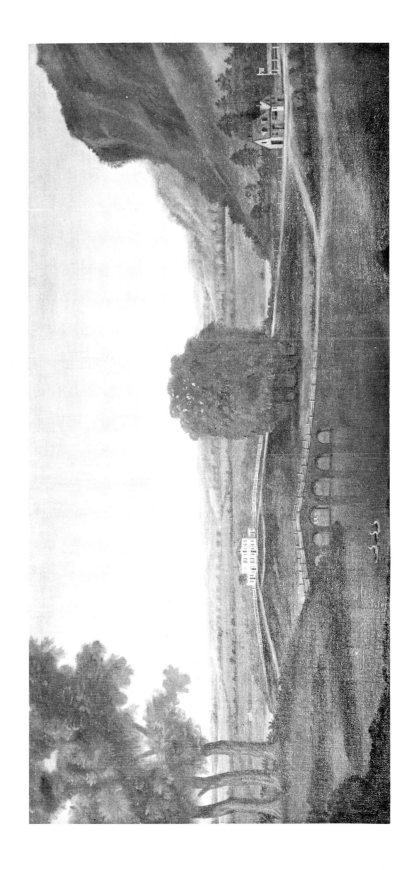

FIGURE 38

BRIGADIER GENERAL GERSHOM BURR
1768-1828

A citizen of prominence in Connecticut, Gershom Burr, son of Gershom Burr, lived at Fairfield. Left fatherless at the age of ten, he was reared by his childless uncle Thaddeus Burr, also of Fairfield, from whom he inherited a large estate. From 1816 to 1824, the sitter served as brigadier general of the militia.

In gray coat and white waistcoat, Burr occupies a coral-red chair. Through the window, Earl shows a bit of Long Island Sound shoreline that has enchanted all who view it. "As charming a glimpse of New England as ever came from his brush," avers Sawitzky[40]; and Flexner[41] writes poetically, "Houses straggle on a promontory under a gray sky enlivened by the flight of birds. A big square-rigger reposes stolidly at its wharf, while tiny men manipulate smaller boats along a sedgy shore."

Since Earl's portrait of the subject's wife, Priscilla Lothrop Burr, is dated 1798, it is assumed that the husband's likeness was painted in the same year.

Unsigned and undated
36 x 33 inches
Mme. Eltore Bottoni
Garches, France

FIGURE 39

THE HONORABLE NOAH SMITH

1754-1838

After graduating from Yale in 1778, Noah Smith, a native of Sheffield, Connecticut, went at once to Bennington, Vermont. In the summer of his arrival, he delivered an address at the first-anniversary observance of the Battle of Bennington. Admitted to the bar in 1779 and serving for some years as state's attorney and county clerk of Bennington County, he was appointed United States Collector of Internal Revenue in 1791. For two years, he was judge of the Supreme Court of Vermont.

The *Noah Smith* is a routine effort typical of Earl's less distinguished output during the later years of the century. Its composition repeats a familiar formula: a figure seated by a table at a window, with books and loops of drapery for backing. Though the set of the head has vitality and the face betrays humor and alertness, there is an over-all lack of finesse in execution.

The map may be recognized as that of Bennington. Among the books are Johnson's *Poets* and Pope's *Iliad*. On the table is a green cloth fringed in gold; under it stands a terrestrial globe. The carpet is multi-colored while the drapery, as usual, is red and gold. Beyond the window, a pinkish landscape stretches away to a single white church spire. The subject, wears a brown suit, white waistcoat, and white clocked hose. That shoemakers of Earl's day made the shoes for both feet virtually alike does not account altogether for the fact that Mr. Smith appears to have interchanged feet.

Signed and dated 1798
64¼ x 42½ inches
The Art Institute of Chicago
Goodman Fund

FIGURE 40

MRS. NOAH SMITH AND HER CHILDREN
1757-1810

Had Charles Willson Peale, Earl's famous contemporary, been commissioned to paint the Smiths, he would probably have grouped them about some center of interest as he did in his well-known conversation piece showing nine members of his own family clustered sociably around a table where a tenth is engaged in sketching. Earl's few group portraits present figures in static line-up, about equally spaced, eyes front. (See Figure 35).

While not the most populous of the artist's canvases—his painting of the Angus Nickelson family portrays nine sitters[42]—the Smith picture is certainly one of the most colorful. The shadows and highlights of Mrs. Smith's glistening gold dress are repeated in the brown coat and yellow breeches and waistcoat of Henry, who stands at left. Daniel, holding a world map, wears rich green; Noah, Jr., fingering grapes from the vine behind him, wears brilliant red. Eliza's white dress is tied with a blue sash, her pink bouquet matching the sash of baby Celia, who is otherwise white-clad. Sofa, chairback, and gold-fringed drapery are all red. The footstool has a green top. Red, blue, green, and yellow combine in the carpet, whose pattern is the same as that in Figure 39. In this spread of vibrant colors, the eye welcomes the passages of white—boot tops, collars, map, caps, dresses, cloak—that are distributed rhythmically across the large canvas.

Mrs. Smith, née Chloe Burrall, was the daughter of Colonel Charles and Abigail (Kellogg) Burrall of Canaan, Connecticut. Henry died young. Daniel entered the ministry and Noah, Jr. teaching. Eliza and Celia married into families residing in Vergennes, Vermont, where they went to live, Celia attaining age seventy-nine.

> Signed and dated 1798
> 64 x 85¾ inches
> The Metropolitan Museum of Art
> New York
> Gift of Edgar William and Bernice Chrysler Garbisch

FIGURE 41

LOOKING EAST FROM DENNY HILL

This large panorama was painted for Colonel Thomas Denny, whose family homestead stood on Denny Hill in the town of Leicester, Massachusetts. When he moved to another residence, he wished to take with him a picture of the view he had known from childhood. Accordingly, Earl was commissioned to record the scene, which he did with fidelity and obvious enjoyment.

The summer landscape stretches to the east. Worcester with its churches lies in the left middle distance, Shrewsbury farther off. The conspicuous road, then the post road between New York and Boston, is now Worcester's main street.

Unlike the *Landscape Painted Near Sharon* (Figure 36), this scene is alive with activity. While tiny mowers lay the grass in windrows at the left, other Lilliputian figures gather it into cocks or load it on an ox-drawn wain. A pair of bulls lock horns in one fenced meadow; sheep cluster on a knoll beyond the center clump of trees. Touched in with the skill of a miniaturist, these engaging details remind one of passages in Pieter Breugel's *Haymaking*, the scene for July in his series of the months.

Although the artist's name and the year 1800 are inscribed in block letters in the lower left corner, it is judged that these are not from Earl's hand and that he produced the picture two or three years earlier.

45¾ x 79⅜ inches
Worcester Art Museum
Worcester, Massachusetts

NOTES

1. Manuscript note accompanying unpublished sketches.

2. Punctuation here added, there being virtually none on the monument.

3. Emory Washburn, *Historical Sketches of the Town of Leicester, Massachusetts, During the First Century of Its Settlement* (Boston, 1860), 61.

4. Alan Burroughs, *Limners and Likenesses: Three Centuries of American Painting* (Cambridge, 1936), 92.

5. Samuel M. Green, "Uncovering the Connecticut School," *Art News*, LI (January, 1953), 38.

6. Cuthbert Lee, *Early American Portrait Painters: The Fourteen Principal Earliest Native-Born Painters* (New Haven, 1929), 211.

7. John Barber and Lemuel S. Punderson, *History and Antiques of New Haven, Connecticut, from Its Earliest Settlement to the Present Time, with Biographical Sketches and Statistical Information of Public Institutions, &c., &c.,* 3rd edition (New Haven, 1870), 157.

8. William Sawitsky, "Ralph Earl's Historical Painting, *A View of the Town of Concord,*" *Antiques*, XXVIII (September, 1935), 98.

9. Barber and Punderson, *op. cit.*

10. Helen Comstock, "Spot News in American Historical Prints, 1755-1800," *Antiques*, LXXX (November, 1961), 446.

11. Thomas H. Gage, "Ralph Earl," *Bulletin of the Worcester Art Museum*, VII (July, 1916), 6-7.

12. John Marshall Phillips, "Ralph Earl, Loyalist," *Art in America*, XXXVII (October, 1949), 187-189.

13. Laurence B. Goodrich, "Ralph Earl's First Royal Academy Entry," *Antiques* LXXV (May, 1959), 456-457.

14. Algernon Graves, *The Royal Academy of Arts: A Complete Dictionary of Contributors and Their Work from Its Foundation in 1769 to 1904* (London, 1905), III, 2.

15. Goodrich, "Ralph Earl's Debt to Gainsborough and Other English Portraitists," *Antiques*, LXXVIII (November, 1960), 464-465.

16. Goodrich, "Ralph Earl's Portraits of Three Young English Ladies," *Antiques*, LXXIV (November, 1958), 418-419.

17. William and Susan Sawitzky, "Two Letters from Ralph Earl with Notes on His English Period," *Worcester Art Museum Annual*, VIII (1960), 8-41.

18. *The Salem Gazette*, May 24, 1785, and *Thomas's Massachusetts Spy*, May 26, 1785. The first entry was discovered by Nina Fletcher Little, who brought it to the attention of W. and S. Sawitzky, in whose study, *op. cit.,* it is reprinted.

19. Henry Marceau, "A Recently Discovered Portrait by Ralph Earl," *Gazette des Beaux-Arts*, XXIII (April, 1943), 251-255.

20. Collected by Rita Susswein Gottesman, *The Arts and Crafts in New York, 1777-1799: Advertisements and News Items from New York City Newspapers* (New York, 1954), 5.

21. James A. Hamilton, *Reminiscences of James A. Hamilton; or, Men and Events, at Home and Abroad, During Three Quarters of a Century* (New York, 1869), 4.

22. William Dunlap, *A History of the Rise and Progress of the Arts of Design in the United States* (New York, 1834).

23. Hugh Dalziel, *British Dogs: Their Varieties, History, Characteristics, Breeding, Management, and Exhibition* (London, 1880), 135.

24. Sir Gyles Isham, Bart., "Correspondence," *Country Life* (May 3, 1956), 934.

25. Tentative identification made after considerable investigation by Helen Davey Hall, formerly Assistant to the Director, Smith College Museum of Art.

26. Robert O. Parks, "Smith College Museum: Recent Accessions," *College Art Journal*, XVII, no. 1 (Fall, 1957), 73-75.

27. Information furnished the author by Count de Salis and confirmed by the following excerpt from *The Family and Heirs of Sir Francis Drake* by Lady Eliott-Drake (London, 1911), II, 323:

    Marianne and Sophy, Admiral William Drake's two daughters, then at school in London, are frequently mentioned as improving in health and accomplishments, and in 1782 we are told that "Sir Francis has taken possession of Magdalen Hill," a place we have been unable to identify, but suppose it must have been in the neighborhood of Kew, and for his use when the court was in residence there.

28. W. Sawitzky, *Connecticut Portraits by Ralph Earl, 1751-1801* (Catalogue for the Connecticut Tercentenary, Yale Gallery of Fine Arts, 1935), 3, 12.

29. W. and S. Sawitzky, *op. cit.*

30. Perry T. Rathbone, "The Seymour Portraits by Ralph Earl," *Bulletin of the City Art Museum of St. Louis*, XXXIV, no. 2 (Spring, 1948), 23.

31. Lucy Tuckerman, "Landscape and Portrait by Ralph Earl," *Worcester Art Bulletin*, VII, no. 4 (January, 1917), 7-10.

32. Rathbone, *op. cit.*, quotes from M. W. Seymour, *Record of the Seymour Family in the Revolution* (privately printed, 1912).

33. Samuel Orcutt, *History of the Towns of New Milford and Bridgewater, Connecticut, 1703-1882* (1882), 774.

34. Homer Saint-Gaudins, *The American Artist and His Times* (New York, 1941), 42.

35. Robert L. Harley, "Ralph Earl, Eighteenth-Century Connecticut Artist, Comes into His Own," *American Collector*, XIV, no. 10 (November, 1945), 10-13.

36. Quoted in full by A. Elizabeth Chase from *Wolcott Memorial* in "Ralph Earl's Portrait of Mrs. Moseley and Her Son Charles," *Bulletin of the Associates in Fine Arts at Yale University*, XII, no. 1 (February, 1943), 1.

37. *The Ellsworth Homestead, Past and Present* (The Connecticut Daughters of the Revolution, 1907).

38. Frederic Fairchild Sherman, "An Early and a Late Portrait by Ralph Earl," *Art in America*, XXIV (April, 1936), 91.

39. Thomas Tileston Waterman, *The Dwellings of Colonial America* (Chapel Hill, 1950), 274.

40. W. Sawitzky, *Ralph Earl, 1751-1801* (Catalogue for exhibitions at the Whitney Museum of American Art and Worcester Art Museum, 1946), entry 46.

41. James Thomas Flexner, *The Light of Distant Skies, 1760-1835* (New York, 1954), 70.

42. Sherman, "The Angus Nickelson Family," *Art in America*, XXIII, (October, 1931), 154-155.